BEYOND THE STATISTICS

Profiles of Ordinary Men of Color Doing
the Extraordinary

By

ZANE M. MASSEY

ISBN: 0615585302
ISBN 13: 9780615585307

Library of Congress Control Number: 2012904602
CreateSpace, North Charleston, SC

ACKNOWLEDGMENTS

I want to thank God for bringing this idea to me. I want to thank my lovely wife for putting up with me every day, I love you; my mother for editing; Ross; Seku; Kwame; Joshua; Wouri; Johnathan; Brian; Humble; and Darren.

I want to thank God for bringing this idea to me. I want to thank my lovely wife for putting up with me every day, I love you; my mother for editing; Ross; Seku; Kwame; Joshua; Wouri; Johnathan; Brian; Humble; and Darren.

CONTENTS

FOREWORD

If there is no struggle, there is no progress.
— FREDERICK DOUGLASS, 1857

These interviews take me back to when I first read *Narrative of the Life of Frederick Douglass: An American Slave*. I was fourteen years old, a freshman in high school, and, for once, I was not the only Black boy in the class. I grew up in a racially mixed family (black mother, white father), but I lived in a mostly white section of Coney Island, Brooklyn; and for elementary and junior high school, my parents bussed me to a mostly white Catholic school in another neighborhood. High school was the first time in my life I learned with (and from) other young black men; the first time I read black poets like Langston Hughes and black intellectual activists like Douglass; the first time I found supportive peers in other black men who were not my cousins. Reading Douglass's *Narrative* in that type of environment changed my life because learning of Douglass's struggle for freedom while experiencing my developing identity as an African-American man inspired me to connect academic excellence to black identity, to see my own personal and professional goals as part of a continuation of Douglass's fight for black humanity and black equality in America and the world.

I feel the same type of motivation and inspiration from reading these interviews. As the title suggests, when it comes to charting a course for black men in America (and the world), we desperately need to go beyond the statistics. Pedro Noguera's book *The Trouble with Black Boys ... And Other Reflections on Race, Equity, and the Future of Public Education* begins with the bleak, but real assessment that "Black males in American society are in trouble. With respect to health, education, employment, income, and overall well-being, all of the most reliable data consistently indicate that black males constitute a segment of the population that is distinguished by hardships, disadvantages, and vulnerability." That is the story of black masculinity we see in numbers on everything from prison population to poverty rates, high school drop outs to AIDS cases. The enormity of the crisis is enough to make anyone want to give up the larger struggles for humanity and decency that our ancestors have been fighting since the Middle Passage.

But that is where these interviews, like Douglass's narrative, become so important. We, as black men, are more than how we appear in statistics and on television. After I read Douglass's narrative, no one—black or white—could tell me that academic success was not in keeping with black traditions, was a form of "acting white." Douglass's life all but told me, "Fool, getting a strong education is the blackest thing you can do!" These interviews say the same thing. And like Douglass, they remind us that success for its own sake, for personal profit and individual advancement, is *not* part of our struggle. If in our achievements we are not giving back to others like us, if we are not paving a way for future people's success, then we have failed to build from past struggles and those struggles will, therefore, be in vain.

I took up the torch that Douglass passed to me by studying history and researching and writing on black political struggles for freedom. I am a teacher and a scholar, and I see it as my life's work to show all my students, but especially my black students, the richness of black history and its unfulfilled legacies. As the statistics indicate, there is much work left undone, and the struggle continues.

The participants in this book share with us many ways everyday black men find and hold on to motivation—from family, community, and history. They are not superstar athletes or musicians; their "ordinariness" is what makes them extraordinary. Douglass, at one point, was also an ordinary black man in Maryland, a slave who one day decided he was going to fight—literally—for his freedom and the freedom of others like him. The fight, the struggle is what made him extraordinary.

The men interviewed here have taken up the same fight—as doctors, teachers, and entrepreneurs. In their own way, they too are extraordinary, because, like Douglass, they see their lives as more devoted to larger principles than just professional or financial success. Their stories show us how they developed that outlook. Their narratives can help us get beyond the statistics and see that we are more than the sum total of data on our crises.

Brian Purnell
Assistant Professor of Africana Studies, Bowdoin College

INTRODUCTION

The phenomenon of racial profiling has recently become better known—but it has long been a part of U.S. culture, as experienced by and as known to African Americans since the days of slavery, when monitoring of the movements of blacks and freed slaves was the norm. But this phenomenon has only recently been acknowledged in the past several years outside of the African American community. —SHUFORD

Starting in the 1980s, the "War on Drugs" was clearly associated with racial profiling. In direct response to the 1980s crack-cocaine epidemic, those conducting the War on Drugs believed that they needed to focus on African Americans and Hispanics, since they were more likely than any other demographic to be carrying drugs. This assumption has been examined in detail and shown to be wrong. African Americans do not transport or use drugs more than anyone else: they use them much the same as other people (Shuford).

Statistics to support these absurd findings are constantly spread throughout all forms of media, particularly during the seven o'clock news. However you will find that, statistically, among those arrested for drug crimes, the prevalence of illegal drug use among white men is *approximately the same* as that among black men, but:

- Black men are five times as likely to be arrested for a drug offense as a white male;
- Half the inmates in the United States are African American;
- One out of every fourteen black men is now in prison or jail;
- One out of every three black men between twenty and twenty-nine years of age is behind bars, on probation, or on parole;
- One out of every four black men is likely to be imprisoned at some point during his lifetime (Schlosser).

However, concerning African-American males and other men of color, a majority of statistics fail to address and celebrate those men who, in spite of insurmountable odds, are able to achieve greatness and contribute invaluable resources to their inner-city communities and to society at large. The latter portion of the twentieth century has unveiled the upwardly mobile black man. Incidence of educated black men has significantly increased and social and political milestones that once seemed out of reach are now achievable. The visible increase in men of color in the areas of business, politics, law, medicine, and many other specialties provide visible proof of the expansion of non-Caucasians in roles that throughout history were typically reserved for white men.

This book will provide an up-close and personal journey into the lives of black men who defied negative statistical analysis. What is about to unfold is the *positive side of racial profiling,* if there has ever been such a term.

CHAPTER 1

BLACK MEN DO TEACH
(There Is Always Someone Out There)

While it is no secret that there is indeed a shortage of quality African American teachers (and quality teachers of all races for that matter), these two brothers, Ross and Seku, are prime examples of the talent that exists in the public school system. These men are young, intelligent, fearless, and uncompromising, but more importantly, they have a beat on what is going on with our youth. I am truly grateful that I went to Clark Atlanta University because it is where I met these two gentlemen—Ross, with a mass media and communications background, and Seku, with a degree in mathematics. Both could be working for any Fortune 500 company in the world right now or even heading up their own businesses, but they chose to serve our young brothers and sisters by attempting to instill the same pride and determination in our children that they embrace.

Both men come from humble beginnings (Queens, Harlem) in New York, but through persistence, patience, and alertness they have been able to rise above the stereotypes often aimed at them. In a world where our culture glamorizes the athlete, entertainer, and "thug," these brothers are welcome changes to these stereotypical images of black men and exhibit the true potentiality of men of color. The beautiful thing is they are young brothers with many years of teaching in front of them, and they will most certainly make a positive impact in the lives of our young ones.

Truth be told, if it was not for my sixth-grade teacher, either I would be dead or—you guessed it—behind bars. My teacher affected my life in such a way that I followed his example and became a teacher because I wanted to make an impact in the same way he did. Sometimes it is a tough job with low pay, but at the end of the day, you know that you made a difference in someone's life. I am proud to say that I still keep in touch with some of my former students who are now adults, and I honestly feel I was able to help them through struggles in their teenage lives just by being there to listen and offer sound advice.

SEKU BRAITHWAITE, EDUCATOR

This is a photo of a tired Seku,
full-time educator, part time prize fighter.

| WHAT IS YOUR AGE?

I am thirty-four.

| WHERE ARE YOU FROM? TELL ME ABOUT
| YOUR "ROOTS."

I was born and raised in Harlem, New York City. My
adolescence was in the '90s, but I do remember some of the

3

'80s, probably more than someone my age should. I suppose it's a result of having five older siblings, four of them brothers. I grew up on the borderline between west Harlem and Spanish Harlem. My parents were both born in the United States, though my father's side of the family is from Barbados. That bit of cultural connection was a footnote, but it didn't define us. I had a pan-African upbringing, meaning we were taught to identify with people of African descent throughout the Diaspora, whether they were in the Caribbean, Africa, the Americas, etc.

WHAT IMPACT DID YOUR LIVING ENVIRONMENT HAVE ON YOUR CHILDHOOD?

It had an enormous impact on me. Everything from where I lived to where I was born in the order of my parents' children has helped shape me. Of course my parents did also, and, though they were not rich financially, they were highly respected and known figures in the community. I also experienced special, unique, and traumatic circumstances that occurred over the course of my adolescence that made me who I am. I had a father who was at the center of numerous cultural and political events concerning African people throughout the Diaspora, which included Nelson Mandela's first visit to Harlem. I had a mother who fought the city and at one point had my older brothers' elementary and middle school shut down due to asbestos contamination. I also received a brutal crash course on how the criminal justice system and news media really work. I witnessed childhood friends from my building and neighboring housing complexes be sent to prison and juvenile facilities for most of their adolescence for a high profile crime (which they were exonerated for more than fifteen years after their convictions). Many, myself included, knew they had not committed the crime.

> DID YOU HAVE A ROLE MODEL OR
> MENTOR AS A CHILD? IF SO, DESCRIBE
> THE LESSONS AND GUIDANCE THAT YOU
> RECEIVED FROM HIM OR HER.

I do not think I had a role model or any single individual that I personally admired. However both my parents were respected and socially and politically active figures in Harlem and the New York City area. In the case of my father, he was also active internationally. His activism was not part of his nine-to-five job, so it was as if he was working two full-time jobs. Even though he was not always around to do many "father and son" activities, his life has served as an example. Also, beyond my parents, I had four older brothers who were generally liked, recognized, and respected in Harlem, and between all of them, I could usually find something worth emulating.

> WHAT IS YOUR CURRENT OCCUPATION?
> DESCRIBE THE STEPS THAT YOU HAD
> TO TAKE TO ARRIVE ON YOUR CURRENT
> CAREER PATH.

After working about seven and a half years as a software engineer for a financial services company, I decided to do something I had been thinking about for a long time. I made a complete career switch and began teaching high school mathematics in the autumn of 2007. My original career path as an engineer served its purpose for that chapter of my life, but I knew it was something I did not want to dedicate my life or most of my waking hours to doing. I felt like I had a lot of talents, insights, and experiences to offer young people, especially those from similar ethnic and socioeconomic backgrounds that could help them successfully navigate their lives into adulthood.

DESCRIBE THE IMPACT THAT EDUCATION HAS HAD ON YOUR LIFE.

The importance of education is a topic that is full of clichés, but honestly many of them are true. I was in and out of elementary and middle school as a child, spending much of that time being homeschooled because my mother was not happy with the educational experiences provided to my older siblings. It is certainly not a path for everyone, but this educational experience led directly to me getting into one of New York City's top public high schools. This positioned me to have a choice of colleges and to attend college and graduate school at virtually no cost to me. Without an education I certainly would not be able to do anything I do, nor have the type of options or control over my life that I have, and I believe having options is critical to one's well-being.

Everyone does not need to go out and get a master's degree or a doctorate or deeply pursue higher education, but more people should than do, especially in the kind of community from which I come. Growing up, many people around me really had unrealistic dreams that far too often revolved around careers in entertainment, and I still see this playing out with the students I teach, but if nothing else, it is good to have an education should you find yourself unsuccessful in pursuing your dream.

Education should never be confused with intelligence. I know many formally educated people who have bachelor's degrees in a variety of areas, but at the end of the day, they really are not very bright or knowledgeable about much, so we should strive to be both educated and intelligent.

IN YOUR OPINION, WHAT IS THE MAIN
ISSUE THAT IS DISTRACTING YOUTH
TODAY FROM ACHIEVING THEIR FULL
POTENTIAL?

I do not know if you can pick one single issue. The pathologies so many of us complain about and shake our heads over that we see manifested in young people in our communities have very good explanations behind them. These youth are usually just products of a society that is completely broken at many levels, and those problems always show up the most pointedly in the most disadvantaged communities. We live in a society whose mantras are based on the philosophy of profit over people, as well as selfishness, and it promotes the myth that everyone can be rich, achieve their dreams, etcetera, when in actuality society is set up to assure the exact opposite outcome. With that stated, I would say one of the biggest issues we are facing is the dissolution of the "family" and the sense of community.

When I say "family," I am not just talking about the standard, textbook, two-parent household because that is certainly not the only way to have a healthy family, but I am talking about the notion of people in communities looking out for each other's children and interests. I just look at some of the differences between the experiences of myself and my older siblings when we were growing up. While my older siblings were growing up, there were still people left in the neighborhood who would tell on you, take you to your parent, or discipline you themselves if they saw you doing something wrong in the street. I think this changed somewhere in the '80s and early '90s as many inner-city communities were dealing with what many call the "crack era." It seems like somewhere around that time something changed in our communities, and our adults became afraid of our children. Consequently many young people do not have the same respect for adults, nor do they look to them as examples.

Also related to this lost sense of community is that many of those who are "successful" are not actively looking to help others or create anything enduring that can help others to enjoy similar success. It seems like many of us just want to do as much as we can to accumulate as many material goods as possible and call it a life. This is a very callous and selfish way of going about life, but it truly epitomizes the "American dream."

WHAT ADVICE DO YOU HAVE FOR A YOUNG PERSON GROWING UP IN TODAY'S WORLD?

My advice to a person growing up in today's world is, "Be the change in the world you wish to see," as Gandhi once said. Be compassionate and empathetic, know that another world is possible, and if you accept those pieces of advice then realize you will probably spend much of your adult life correcting the mistakes of the adults who have come before you—maybe even your parents.

WERE THERE ANY OBSTACLES IN YOUR LIFE THAT YOU HAD TO OVERCOME? HOW DID YOU HURDLE THEM?

Well in my community growing up, peer pressure, drugs, pregnancy, and violence were always just a short distance away, but at the same time there was also hope and love. I don't feel my obstacles were any larger than those of most people who grew up in similar communities, ethnically and socio-economically. In fact, my obstacles were probably a lot smaller because, despite having similar circumstances, I had fully present parents, a very supportive family, good examples, and a bevy of family and friends who had extremely high expectations for me. Sure this made for added pressure on me, but in many ways it led to me feeling throughout my life that failure just was not an option.

| WHAT DOES FAMILY MEAN TO YOU?

More than the obvious meaning of those whom you are biologically related to, "family" can be those people in your inner circle. Family can be the people you share an extended close relationship with, or really whomever you decide is your family. But they should be people who are truly supportive of you, love you without condition, and can be counted on in a time of crisis or difficulty. You can't control what group of people you were born into, but you do control which friends you select.

| HOW DO YOU GIVE BACK TO YOUR
| COMMUNITY?

Currently I primarily give back through my profession, which is teaching, though this certainly isn't the only way. When I started teaching I especially wanted to work with high school youth for all the reasons previously mentioned. I felt I could make the biggest impact and be the most effective working with that age group. In the future I plan to stay in some form of education and work with or for young people. It might not be as lucrative as my previous career, but I find it a lot more fulfilling and rewarding in other ways.

| WHAT IS YOUR PHILOSOPHY ON LIFE?

Wow, I have many philosophies on life, some of them very specific. I'm not going to list them all though, so I guess I will choose the most important one, and that is the very ancient "golden rule": do unto others as you would have them do unto you. It sounds really simple, but if people really lived by it just imagine how much better a place the world would be.

Seku - educating the youth.

Ross T. Hamilton, Jr., educator

Educator Ross Hamilton (striped shirt)
pauses to take a picture with his class.

| WHAT IS YOUR AGE?

I was born September 18, 1978. So that makes me a young
thirty-four.

WHERE ARE YOU FROM? TELL ME ABOUT YOUR "ROOTS."

I am a native New Yorker, born in Queens (East Elmhurst) and raised in New Rochelle. Although I was raised in New York, I have also lived in Atlanta, Newark, and Jersey City, and I currently reside in Philadelphia. All of these cities have played a part in shaping the person that I am today.

WHAT IMPACT DID YOUR LIVING ENVIRONMENT HAVE ON YOUR CHILDHOOD?

Growing up in a city with a diverse population such as New Rochelle has had a tremendous impact on my psyche. While growing up in New Rochelle, I had many friends of different nationalities and faiths. This enabled me to learn at a very early age that we live in a global society. Due to this I have always been respectful of other cultures and beliefs that may be foreign to me. In addition, the outstanding educational foundation that I received at school was reinforced at home. My parents have always pushed me to strive for success in all of my endeavors, whether it was in athletics, school, or music. My mother and father were both pianists, so they pushed me to expand my musical knowledge by enrolling me in piano lessons and taking me to Broadway plays. The supportive foundation that I had outside of school was instrumental in aiding my performance as a student.

| DID YOU HAVE A ROLE MODEL OR
| MENTOR AS A CHILD? IF SO, DESCRIBE
| THE LESSONS AND GUIDANCE THAT YOU
| RECEIVED FROM HIM OR HER.

My maternal grandfather, Joseph Plaskett, was my mentor and role model as a youth. My grandfather, whom my family referred to as "Pop-Pop," was a successful businessman who created the renowned Hairstyling by Joseph, a high-end beauty salon located in midtown Manhattan. Hairstyling by Joseph is one of the few upscale beauty salons in midtown, completely owned and operated by African Americans. I can vividly recall the long talks that Pop-Pop had with me when I was a teenager, in which he instilled in me the importance of education and family. It was my grandfather who kept reminding me that alcohol and drugs could easily sidetrack a person from achieving success in life. Even though my grandfather passed away in 2003, I still utilize his words in guiding my life today.

| WHAT IS YOUR CURRENT OCCUPATION?
| DESCRIBE THE STEPS THAT YOU HAD
| TO TAKE TO ARRIVE ON YOUR CURRENT
| CAREER PATH.

I am a high school social studies teacher for the Philadelphia school district. Prior to working in Philadelphia, I taught for three years in the New York City school system at an expeditionary learning high school in the Bronx.

In 2000 I graduated from Clark Atlanta University with a degree in mass media arts. After working for six years in the media industry, I decided to pursue a career in education. I enrolled in a graduate program at St. John's University, where I obtained my master's degree in adolescent education in 2007.

DESCRIBE THE IMPACT THAT EDUCATION HAS HAD ON YOUR LIFE.

Education has provided me with a wonderful teaching career, endless opportunities to travel, a network of friends, and a family. Yes, it was at Clark Atlanta University where I courted a fellow student named Imani who eventually became my wife. Education has been an essential key in opening numerous doors in my life.

IN YOUR OPINION, WHAT IS THE MAIN ISSUE THAT IS DISTRACTING YOUTH TODAY FROM ACHIEVING THEIR FULL POTENTIAL?

I believe that the youth of today are fixated on attaining a large amount of wealth with little to no effort. It appears that the compass guiding our youth today is money. Today's media has reinforced this ideology by airing reality shows that display wealthy celebrities who wantonly disregard their finances. This ideology is in direct conflict with the concept of college, where one spends several years in class to obtain a degree that may not produce immediate wealth. To combat this issue, parents need to turn off these shows and talk to their kids. These talks can be centered on how a college degree can impact not only themselves, but also their families, communities, and the world!

WHAT ADVICE DO YOU HAVE FOR A YOUNG PERSON GROWING UP IN TODAY'S WORLD?

My advice would be to seek an internship and/or a mentor in the career or field that you are interested in pursuing. If you have an opportunity to get a part-time job, then do it. It is important to begin working at an early age, because it builds discipline, independence, and work experience, and it is an opportunity to learn how to manage your finances. Lastly I strongly believe that you must have some element of faith instilled in your life. The road to success is a rocky one, and it is important that you have some element of faith to lean on when the storms do arise.

WERE THERE ANY OBSTACLES IN YOUR LIFE THAT YOU HAD TO OVERCOME? HOW DID YOU HURDLE THEM?

When I was fifteen, my father was incarcerated. As a result of this event, my family, which included my mother, brother, and sister, were split apart into different living situations. Although this was a traumatic event, it actually brought me closer to my extended family. It was the love and support that I received from my grandparents, uncles, aunts, and cousins that allowed me to survive my darkest hour and be the man I am today.

| WHAT DOES FAMILY MEAN TO YOU?

Family is the bedrock of my life. I learned this through the support that I received as a youth and even today as an adult. In 2007 my wife and I became the proud parents of a beautiful daughter named Anaya. It is through the support of my wife and daughter that I am able to survive the most stressful of days. My wife and I have made it a point to introduce my daughter to all of her extended family so that she can also appreciate the importance of a strong family bond.

| HOW DO YOU GIVE BACK TO YOUR
| COMMUNITY?

I give back to my community every day through educating the youth and aiming them toward success. During the historic presidential election of 2008, my fraternity brothers and I were in the Jersey City, New Jersey, community registering people to vote as part of a Phi Beta Sigma Fraternity, Inc. registration drive. Being active in a graduate chapter provides me with the platform to create opportunities to positively impact my community while working alongside likeminded professional men.

| WHAT IS YOUR PHILOSOPHY ON LIFE?

Tackle life with one hand stretched north and the other south. The northern hand should always be focused on pulling yourself higher, while the southern hand is always ready to help others reach your level.

CHAPTER 2

IS THERE A DOCTOR IN THE HOUSE?

(That's My Best Friend)

Many inner-city schools have one room or area where the students eat lunch, have gym, and put on school plays and other events. That place is known as the cafégymtorium. At my grammar school the cafégymtorium was the place where individual academic rewards were handed out. One afternoon we had an assembly where students from first to eighth grades were being honored for grades above 95 percent (first honors) and above 85 percent (second honors).

Kwame Ohemeng, one of my best friends and brothers to this day, received first honors for his outstanding academic performance in the third grade. It always seemed that he was six foot and five inches tall, even though we were in the third grade. Kwame had the longest arms and legs I had ever seen on a third-grader. In all fairness I'll just say Kwame was awkward. Nevertheless, as awkward as he was, he was every bit as bright, and I wanted to be as smart as he was. In fact from third to eighth grade, we maintained a friendly rivalry—not a rivalry to see who the best basketball player was (as I was clearly superior in that), but a rivalry to see who was the smartest student in the school. Throughout the course of those five years, I would say it was a tie, but when we all got to high school, Kwame surpassed me in academic prowess. I still tried and did the best I could. That is what true friendship is all about.

The moral of the story here is that when picking friends (Kwame and I have been best friends for over twenty years), aspire to befriend someone who has a particular strength that you do not have. There is always someone who is more outgoing or more intelligent than you. Pick friends who have positive qualities that you can benefit from. Even though Kwame and I were materially poor, our friendship is, and always has been, very rich. When our fathers weren't there at times to give us the needed encouragement or advice, I felt that we were there for each other.

So it really does not matter where you started; it is where you are going that really matters. The most effective way to go somewhere in life is to be accompanied by good, positively motivated people. If you don't have a Kwame in your life, seek him out; read about him. Get something positive going in your life. Leave people alone who have nothing going for themselves, who speak negatively about self and others, and who do things that hurt themselves and others. It's OK to try and raise your brother up and "drop some knowledge," but if they dismiss your attempts to help, leave them alone. You are not for them and they are not for you. If it was not for Dr. Kwame Ohemeng, I would not be able to see the greatness in myself. To me, he is more than a friend. He is my big brother, mentor and a father figure rolled up into one. Recently, Kwame got married, and I was honored to be his best man throughout the wedding ceremony. As his bride-to-be walked down the Church aisle, all I could think to myself was how thankful I am to be a part of this ceremony and to have had such an impactful friend that continues to push me forward, always for the better.

KWAME A. OHEMENG, M.D.

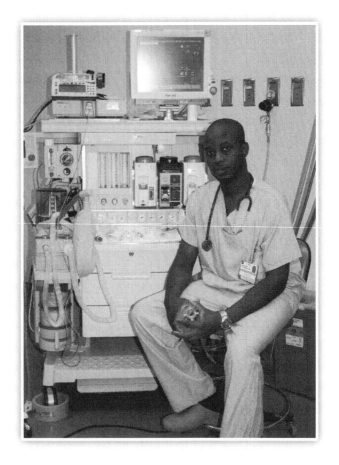

Dr. Kwame Ohemeng, just before surgery. What a pair of hands.

| WHAT IS YOUR AGE?

I'm thirty-four.

| WHERE ARE YOU FROM? TELL ME
| ABOUT YOUR "ROOTS."

I was born and raised in Harlem. However, my roots are in Ghana. Both of my parents are from Ghana.

| WHAT IMPACT DID YOUR LIVING
| ENVIRONMENT HAVE ON YOUR
| CHILDHOOD?

I grew up in a pretty full house. My mother and I lived in an apartment with my grandma, my cousin, my uncle, my aunt, and her husband. Having my extended family there was a source of discipline and gave me strong male role models to look up to.

| DID YOU HAVE A ROLE MODEL OR
| MENTOR AS A CHILD? IF SO, DESCRIBE
| THE LESSONS AND GUIDANCE THAT
| YOU RECEIVED FROM HIM OR HER.

I was fortunate to have several role models growing up. The most important one had to be my mom. The lesson she taught me is that you should always strive to leave a place better off than when you got there. For her this meant I had better not make a mess when we go to someone's house

23

to visit. I extrapolated this to my general philosophy on life. My goal is to make an impact on the people I come in contact with. I hope to have a positive impact on their lives. I also learned from her my mom's selflessness. She sacrificed so much so that I could have a good education.

WHAT IS YOUR CURRENT OCCUPATION? DESCRIBE THE STEPS THAT YOU HAD TO TAKE TO ARRIVE ON YOUR CURRENT CAREER PATH.

I am an anesthesiologist. The steps I have had to take are numerous. Aside from the twenty-plus years of schooling (yes, I said twenty-plus!), I have had to sacrifice time and personal relationships in pursuit of my dream. In high school I volunteered in an emergency room. In college I participated in summer enrichment courses at the University of Connecticut. Following graduation I spent a year doing clinical research. It has not been an easy road, but I would not change a thing.

DESCRIBE THE IMPACT THAT EDUCATION HAS HAD ON YOUR LIFE.

Education was not an option in my family. There was no question of *if* you were going to college. The question was where you were going. Education was the means of escape from poverty and how I could give my mom the kind of life she deserves. Education has allowed me to interact and exchange ideas with people from all over the world. I cannot begin to describe the impact it has had on my life.

> **IN YOUR OPINION, WHAT IS THE MAIN ISSUE THAT IS DISTRACTING TODAY'S YOUTH FROM ACHIEVING THEIR FULL POTENTIAL?**

BET. Not exactly, I guess. However, I believe there is a lack of patience in today's youth. In the words of rapper Drake, they want the money, cars, clothes, hoes, etcetera, and they want them now. They are not willing to put in the time and effort to earn those things. They want them to fall into their laps. This can be blamed, in part, on the images of black success that they see on television. The people that have the things they lust for are entertainers and sports figures. They fail to see the black physicians, lawyers, businessmen, etc. who earned those things with hard work, sacrifice, and education.

> **WHAT ADVICE DO YOU HAVE FOR A YOUNG PERSON GROWING UP IN TODAY'S WORLD?**

The only thing that you can acquire in this life that cannot be taken away from you is education. Material things can be lost in an instant, but education is eternal.

WERE THERE ANY OBSTACLES IN YOUR LIFE THAT YOU HAD TO OVERCOME? HOW DID YOU HURDLE THEM?

There have definitely been obstacles in my life. I had to overcome the hurt, anger, and lack of self-esteem that comes from growing up without a father in your life. I overcame these through my relationship with Jesus Christ. I learned that I could get the things I was missing from an earthly father from my Heavenly Father. Studying the Word showed me how He sees me, and the good things that he desires for my life. It also allowed me to forgive my father, thus freeing me from the weight of anger and unforgiveness.

WHAT DOES FAMILY MEAN TO YOU?

Family means everything to me. Family is that support net that allows you to fully grow into who you are. They allow you to experiment and take risks, knowing that they'll be there to catch you when you mess up.

HOW DO YOU GIVE BACK TO YOUR COMMUNITY?

I mentor medical students who may be struggling during their preclinical and clinical years. I also sponsor students in Ghana who cannot afford to pay for schooling.

| WHAT IS YOUR PHILOSOPHY ON LIFE?

Always leave a place better off than when you got there. My other is, "The only thing that can make a dream impossible to achieve is the fear of failure."

CHAPTER 3

THE SPIRIT OF ENTREPRENEURSHIP

(Invest In Yourself)

The term "hater" is defined as a person or group of persons who try to discourage someone from attaining a goal in an effort to inflict their self-imposed limitations on another. In other words, the hater feels that because he or she cannot do something, you shouldn't be able to do it either.

Well, Joshua Woods and Wouri Vice are here to tell you something different. "Haters" have tried to stop them time and time again from reaching their goals, but they constantly succeeded in their respective missions by side-stepping or simply running over those that opposed them. These two young entrepreneurs are crafting their ways to stardom, as they bring their ideas and dreams into reality. Armed with a confident-but-humble swagger and a spiritual presence, these men were able to overcome the limitations that "haters" tried to place on them.

I met Joshua at the Franciscan Community Center, a place where my friends and I escaped from the world to play hoops after school for a couple of hours each week. Thinking back, I realize how blessed we were to have such a safe haven that allowed us to not be in the streets, possibly getting into trouble that we could not see. I remember Josh, who is several years younger than I, wanting to always play basketball with the older teens. As sixteen year olds, when the younger teens played with us, we would always elbow them and trash talk with them. Surviving this physical and mental test was and is still seen as "a rite of passage" on the basketball court. If you endured, then you could always play with the big kids. Some kids would leave the community center in frustration, failing to past the test to make it as a player in our community center. Joshua, however, was always aggressive and tried to hold his own when playing with us. Perhaps this tenacity is the main reason why he has become such a successful entrepreneur in the world of apparel and accessories, some fifteen years later.

JOSHUA WOODS, ENTREPRENEUR

Joshua Woods, a young mogul in the making.

| WHAT IS YOUR AGE?

I'm currently twenty-seven years old.

| WHERE ARE YOU FROM? TELL ME
| ABOUT YOUR "ROOTS."

I was born, raised, and still reside in Harlem. I am rooted in the South Bronx, New York City, on my mother's side, and Monroe, Louisiana, on my father's side. My grandparents were from Humacao, the east end of Puerto Rico, and Central Monroe, Louisiana. My great grandparents were from Galicia, Spain, on my mother's side and from Virginia, on my father's side.

| WHAT IMPACT DID YOUR LIVING
| ENVIRONMENT HAVE ON YOUR
| CHILDHOOD?

Growing up in Harlem was rough. There was a lot of peer pressure everywhere. In addition to that, I was raised in a single-parent household with three other siblings. Nevertheless, amidst the environment and my dad's absence, Mom always had us in good spirits, which was the key to sustaining my confidence. We lived a humble, middle-class lifestyle but with our spirits set on high. I was always content with any situation and still remain that way today.

DID YOU HAVE A MENTOR OR A ROLE
MODEL AS A CHILD? IF SO, DESCRIBE
THE LESSONS AND GUIDANCE THAT
YOU RECEIVED FROM HIM OR HER.

My role model was my second to oldest brother for a short while. He was the first one to go to college in my immediate family. He went away to school in Florida and eventually moved to the Cayman Islands with his girlfriend, now wife. I thought that was pretty profound, him making these big leaps, so that motivated me to go to college. However, as I began to get older, the simple motivation of my brother's endeavors dwindled away as I looked to the streets for motivation, like many young men of color do today.

So I looked to the streets for guidance, and I found it. That's what led me to the lifestyle of selling drugs and disobeying the law, which resulted in me getting into many life threatening situations. Even though I had two older brothers, I never had a male figure in my life to help guide me in the right direction; I had to figure it out on my own.

The influence of my mom's church involvement and my reunion with a longtime neighborhood friend helped me choose to leave the streets behind, which ultimately led me to God. I realized that my "friends" on the street corners were wasting their time and that they would eventually end up dead or in jail. It dawned on me that I could do something different and purposeful with my life. By the grace of God, I successfully went on to college and graduated with a bachelor's degree in business management.

WHAT IS YOUR CURRENT
OCCUPATION? DESCRIBE THE STEPS
THAT YOU HAD TO TAKE TO ARRIVE
ON YOUR CURRENT CAREER PATH.

I work in the capacity of a full-time photographer
(joshuawoodsphotography.com) and menswear designer.
The name of my line is called Virile and can be found on
my online store as well as several boutiques in the U.S.
and Europe. In addition to photography and designing,
I also run a successful blog called "in" which highlights
my favorite fabrics, components, and pictures from many
different artists and designers from around the world.

It all really started at church for me. I really didn't know
what it was that I wanted to do; it wasn't until I started
hanging around young professionals and people on the path
of righteousness that I arrived at my place. One thing that
I can say is that I was successful because I sought God first,
and in seeking him, business ideas, wisdom, visions, and
partnerships were all birthed. I believe God gives us our
desires and in that he's allowed me to see certain things to
motivate me and to pursue what it is that's on my heart.

DESCRIBE THE IMPACT THAT
EDUCATION HAS HAD ON YOUR LIFE.

As a young professional in today's world, I have developed
a certain awareness that many of my peers have yet to
attain. I'm not bragging; my awareness is due to my
desire to beat the existing stereotype that is often placed
on young men of color. We are much more than drug
dealers, rappers, and athletes. I graduated in the lower

percentile of my class and did not get accepted to any of the colleges I applied for. That was tough for me and, in essence, it took a bit of my confidence away. But I am living proof that it does not have to end that way. You can always make a positive change in your life as long as you are still alive and breathing.

Later on, I finally decided to take school seriously and started to apply myself more than ever. I applied to and qualified for a small private college and developed into a bookworm in my later years. I then matured into a well-polished young man, and the respect I was receiving from my classmates and professors made me realize that this was the course I wanted to stay on.

Education has equipped me with the appropriate foundation to establish myself as a young professional. Much of the younger generation looks at education as a waste of time, but in fact it's the total opposite. It's one of the biggest investments a young person can make today.

IN YOUR OPINION, WHAT IS THE MAIN ISSUE THAT IS DISTRACTING TODAY'S YOUTH FROM ACHIEVING THEIR FULL POTENTIAL?

I believe there is too much peer pressure, and it is distracting our youth from achieving their fullest potential. The constant battles over who has the best outfits, or who has the freshest sneakers, or even who has the most money not only keep children in bondage to one another, but they distract kids' minds from school work and home activities. It's pretty devastating. I enjoy nice cloths and new sneakers but I don't let it define me. I believe that we should be ourselves and not allow ourselves to be pressured into being something we are not. At the same time, we need to respect the different thoughts and personalities of our peers.

WHAT ADVICE DO YOU HAVE FOR A YOUNG PERSON IN TODAY'S WORLD?

Whatever you do in life, DO NOT do it half-heartedly or with a "just-to-get-by" mentality. Do it with heart and strive for excellence; you will see the difference. A pastor named Jesse Duplantis said, "The poorest person in the world isn't the one without a nickel, it's the one without a dream." Dream and dream big, no matter how young or old you are. Get out of your comfortable situation and challenge yourself physically, mentally, and spiritually. A positive mouth will cause positive living. The streets have a set itinerary for becoming successful. I've tried it, and I am here to tell you that it does not work! Most importantly remember that change starts with you, and you too can go beyond the statistics.

WERE THERE ANY OBSTACLES IN YOUR LIFE THAT YOU HAD TO OVERCOME? HOW DID YOU HURDLE THEM?

While growing up I was very soft-spoken and not confident in my speech. My words would not get across to people, and as a result I would always be left with my words unheard or disregarded.

Finding God enabled me to have more confidence in my speech. I began to speak up for myself, and my words were clearer. As a result my confidence increased, and it has allowed me to excel in job interviews, open discussions, and intense conversations.

| WHAT DOES FAMILY MEAN TO YOU?

I am fortunate to have close ties with my family. It is a sad reality that many children around the world are abandoned or left in orphanages. It was not until recently that I looked at the traditional family structure and realized how important it is for a child's future. Nowadays our society is dealing with uninformed parents and unsatisfactory educational systems. Generational woes do exist, and if a solid foundation is not provided, statistically, you're going to inadvertently deal with a misguided child and, eventually, a misguided adult. Understanding that and looking at how children benefit from a dual-parent household have given me a clear understanding of what a family structure should consist of.

I enjoy my family and all the similar yet different personalities that exist amongst us. Living in a fast-paced environment, it is crucial that you balance your time accordingly. Family means time, undivided time. The serenity that comes from throwing the football around with my nephew or even jumping rope with my niece gives me a warm feeling like no other.

HOW DO YOU GIVE BACK TO YOUR COMMUNITY?

I give back to my community by volunteering my time to shelters around New York City and talking to the residents to encourage them, I also visit youth detention centers twice a year to inspire adolescent inmates, and in addition to that I also volunteer in the outreach ministry at my church once a month.

WHAT IS YOUR PHILOSOPHY ON LIFE?

Not to look down on others unless I am picking them up.

WOURI VICE, CELEBRITY STYLIST/ ENTREPRENEUR

Wouri and I were introduced through a mutual cousin who thought it would be cool for us to meet because we pledged the same collegiate fraternity, Phi Beta Sigma Fraternity, Inc. I can't remember how we are all related, but the most important thing is that Wouri and I had more in common than just our fraternity, He had the coolest personality and was easy to hang out with. Additionally, Wouri and I shared a common drive and passion for success. For as long as I've known Wouri, he has always been determined to be a mogul in fashion and entertainment. Currently, he is living his dream as stylist/fashion consultant to the stars and his career is blossoming beyond his wildest dreams, having the opportunity to work with veteran actresses such as Kerry Washington and Taraji P. Henson and sensational recording artists Elle Varner and Alicia Keys, just to name a few. Below, Wouri Vice will share insight with you on how he has been able to achieve and maintain success in such a challenging industry.

Stylist to the stars, doing what he does best, smiling for the camera.

| **WHAT IS YOUR AGE?**

I'm thirty-three years old.

| **WHERE ARE YOU FROM? TELL ME
| ABOUT YOUR "ROOTS."**

I was born and raised in New York, New York. I am the oldest of mom's four kids, second oldest of my father's four kids. I come from a close-knit family. My mother, grandmother, and stepfather raised us. My parents always made sure there was enough physical and intellectual space for each of us to have freedom of thought and freedom in the physical sense.

| **WHAT IMPACT DID YOUR LIVING
| ENVIRONMENT HAVE ON YOUR
| CHILDHOOD?**

I came from a house of encouragement. My mother always encouraged me to experience things outside of my living environment. She would encourage us to go to plays, musicals, and other events outside of the norm for our neighborhood. Having a culturally aware mother who was in tune with New York society enabled me to be the social savant that I am today. It gave me the knowledge and confidence to be around people of all cultures and appreciate them.

DID YOU HAVE A MENTOR OR A ROLE
MODEL AS A CHILD? IF SO, DESCRIBE
THE LESSONS AND GUIDANCE THAT
YOU RECEIVED FROM HIM OR HER.

Not so much as a child. I guess you could say I was a
pretty free kid. I was kind of in my own space, and I
never really dealt with any other adults outside of my
core family (mother, grandmother, stepfather, aunt). I
did, however, gain some valuable traits from one of my
high school teachers, Ms. Aziza. She was a very humble
person and was a believer in all things. To her nothing
was impossible. She had a knack for knowing what
talent God had given us. Through her I learned two
qualities: perseverance and humility. I was able to put
these two principles into action as an adult. So whatever
task comes my way, whether it's work or personal, I
always strive to persevere and I am humbled by the
power of God.

WHAT IS YOUR CURRENT
OCCUPATION? DESCRIBE THE STEPS
THAT YOU HAD TO TAKE TO ARRIVE
ON YOUR CURRENT CAREER PATH.

I am a fashion stylist and clothing designer. God laid
down an incredible road for me to reach the ultimate
levels of personal and professional success. I was blessed
to obtain an internship with Giorgio Armani through a
college friend who was working there at the time. From

that experience, I was able to gain business knowledge and establish the blueprint for how I wanted to run my own company. Equally as important, that internship taught me how to maintain a professional attitude no matter the circumstances. In this line of work, you encounter a variety of complex personalities; patience is critical. Attending FIT (Fashion Institute of Technology) enabled me to utilize my talent. Believing in myself and staying focused brought me to where I am today.

DESCRIBE THE IMPACT THAT
EDUCATION HAS HAD ON YOUR LIFE.

Honestly, it really had no direct impact on my life, as far as academics go. Everything that has happened to me in life and in my career came from God. I went to school to be social, and that is where I learned how to talk to anyone. I learned how not to be afraid to talk to people. Some people do not gain this skill until adulthood, or ever; I gained this skill while in school.

IN YOUR OPINION, WHAT IS THE MAIN
ISSUE THAT IS DISTRACTING YOUTH
TODAY FROM ACHIEVING THEIR FULL
POTENTIAL?

The media: it presents conflicting ideals and ideologies to our youth. The media has totally stopped pushing education. Now it is focusing on the latest material item. Television, in general, is more violent and totally moving away from morality, values, and who we are supposed to be, which is encouragers to one another.

From 1992 to 1996 television, even though it contained violence and was sexually suggestive, was different than today. Everything on the screen is more visible: sex and violence, in whole, are much more graphic. It makes it easier for our youth to engage in these activities, because it is more vivid. Even looking at the television sets, high definition televisions make the negativity more visual and tangible than it was just a few short years ago. In addition, the fact that information (the Internet, Pay-Per-View TV, movies, and etcetera) is so readily available poses additional threats to our youth. Combined with the lack of parenting, the future seems bleak.

In the '90s my parents were my uncles, aunts, friends' parents—the whole community. I could bring my friends home; my mother knew who my friends were. Today when I talk to my mom—who is fifty-five years old and raising my sixteen-year-old sister—we talk about the differences between raising me and raising her. When I was a teen, the cell phone was not as popular as it is today. Therefore when one of my friends would call the house, there was a good chance they were going to reach my mother on the phone. The most we had were pagers back in those days (seems like so long ago). Today all the kids have iPhones and BlackBerrys. Then you have social networking sites like Twitter and Instagram that everyone is on; it's crazy! Unless you have the CIA on your side, you cannot keep up with whom your kids are interacting with these days. Perfect example: my sister had a "sweet sixteen" party, and out of those one hundred guests, my mother and I probably knew sixteen of them!

Another obstacle is that there is no trust between the youth and their parents. Parents and elders must try to develop trust between them and the next generation so that those who have been there, so to speak, can help their children make decisions in their young adult lives. If trust exists then there can be at least a somewhat stable relationship between parent and child. Times are different now for our kids, and they need the adults' ears. As adults we need to listen more to our kids. This is the main reason why my sister talks to me more than our mother. I listen to her, and this develops the trust in our relationship. She feels as though she can relate to me because I try to relate to her. We must become more flexible with our kids.

WHAT ADVICE DO YOU HAVE FOR A YOUNG PERSON IN TODAY'S WORLD?

Stay off drugs! Just joking. No, for real, stay off drugs!

Exercise all resources to achieve all dreams. That means that *nothing is impossible*. Everything is at your fingertips. If you can get on the Internet to watch a video or download the latest Jay-Z album, then you can research grants and scholarships.

WERE THERE ANY OBSTACLES IN YOUR LIFE THAT YOU HAD TO OVERCOME? HOW DID YOU HURDLE THEM?

My only obstacle was not believing in myself. I had to learn to believe in myself and not let anything stop me.

WHAT DOES FAMILY MEAN TO YOU?

Family means support, love, comfort, balance, and caring. Family doesn't have to be blood, either. If you can find those values in a person, then they are family.

HOW DO YOU GIVE BACK TO YOUR COMMUNITY?

I take the kids from my neighborhood that are interested in fashion and give them opportunities to intern for me. That way they can see this as a realistic goal if they choose to pursue this line of work. I just want to try to keep our youth "faith" based. They have been through so much, and so many are not believers in anything—in God, themselves, nothing—so I try to pull them up and encourage them.

WHAT IS YOUR PHILOSOPHY ON LIFE?

Be happy. I know it seems too simple, but that's really when the blessings come. If you put yourself in the right frame of mind, you will be surprised by what comes your way.

CHAPTER 4

LORD OF THE RINGLING

(Anything Is Possible)

t's hard to believe that segregation legally ended in 1954 with a series of Supreme Court decisions surrounding *Brown vs. Board of Education*. The fact that we are only fifty-eight years removed from that decision is scary. It lets me know that the United States and the rest of the world still have a lot more work to do. The evidence of progress, however, is measurable. We live in a time where an increased number of non-Caucasians have access to higher education, hold positions of power and prestige, and have the freedom to go anyplace in the universe.

During President Barack Obama's address at the NAACP's one-hundredth anniversary, he let the masses know that racism is no excuse for personal failure. While it helps to have been given the context in order to succeed (i.e. access to better education, health care, etcetera), in this day and age, anything is possible, and you can become anything you want to be.

Johnathan Lee Iverson is a prime example of that mantra. With the intellect of a Harvard lawyer—or Howard, for that matter—Iverson chose a non-conventional route to success. He is the youngest and first African American ringmaster of Ringling Bros. and Barnum & Bailey Circus and has been featured as one of Barbara Walters' *10 Most Fascinating People in the World.* But more importantly, you would never know by the way he carries himself that Johnathan is a part of American history. Even more important than that is how devoted he is to his family and his community.

For me, the most compelling thing about Johnathan was that he lived around the corner from me! I used to hang out in front of his building with my friends Derrick, Jason, Jamil and Caesar, who lived in the building and around the neighborhood. As teens, we would stand in front of "the building" for hours, talking about girls who passed by, basketball, sneakers, etc. – all of the stuff that most inner-city teenage boys would generally talk about. Johnathan would come in and out of the building, and would converse with us from time to time. Back then, I didn't know much about him other than that he was a tall guy (about 6'5") and seemed to have a very easygoing personality. Initially, I thought he was a basketball player or something of the like. He was a couple of years older than us and always seemed to be on-the-go, never conversing with us for more than ten minutes at a time. One day while I was talking with my boys, Johnathan came out of the apartment building, said hello to everyone, and kept it moving. Always curious about what Johnathan did with his life, I asked the fellas, "What's the deal with him; does he play ball or something?" The group laughed, and collectively let me know that he was far from a hoops player. They informed me that he was in the theatre arts and was the Ringmaster of Ringling Bros. Circus! When I found this out, it renewed my conviction that anyone can become "somebody," no matter where he or she comes from. (Of course, the fact is that whether our faces are known to the world or whether our own mothers don't know us, we are still "somebody.") Truly Johnathan's story speaks to the saying that "anything is possible." Logically, when I had the idea for this book, I reached out to Johnathan with the help of my friend Jason, and he happily agreed to work with me in this endeavor.

JOHNATHAN LEE IVERSON, RINGMASTER OF RINGLING BROS. AND BARNUM & BAILEY CIRCUS

The youngest and first African-American Ringmaster of
Ringling Brothers Circus

| WHAT IS YOUR AGE?

I'm thirty-six.

WHERE ARE YOU FROM? TELL ME ABOUT YOUR "ROOTS."

I'm from New York City, specifically from the Upper West Side of Manhattan. My mother is from Arkansas and my father was from Trinidad. Everything for me, however, is based in New York. My upbringing could be considered a miracle: my mom, a single parent, raised my brother and me on a postal worker's salary, sending us to private school. We should not have been living on Central Park West! My life was predictable until the age of eleven—home, school, church, repeat. It wasn't until Christmas of 1987 that I found the Boys' Choir of Harlem (BCH) on *60 Minutes*. That is when my life began. My God-brother was in the BCH at the time, so I went there with him, auditioned, and got in. In terms of travel and life, this opened up a whole new world for me.

WHAT IMPACT DID YOUR LIVING ENVIRONMENT HAVE ON YOUR CHILDHOOD?

Access! If I wanted to go out and play I had all of Central Park and its myriad of playgrounds at my disposal. If I wanted to expand my mind, the library was a mere four blocks away. I was afforded a quality education. I was surrounded by a community of family, teachers, and mentors who seemed to have a stake in my development. In this respect I was excessively blessed. My environment afforded me a dual education.

I attended Fiorello H. LaGuardia High School of Music & Art and Performing Arts. As a member of the

Boys Choir of Harlem, I was exposed to a world beyond my own. I was traveling the world at thirteen years old, performing music from every conceivable genre, be it baroque or hip-hop.

However, my greatest education came from my mother. When you consider the fact that you cannot choose your parents, I consider myself enormously blessed to have the family that I have. My mother is the greatest thing to ever happen to me. She set the foundation for my life as it is and as it shall be. Despite the handicap of single parenthood, we managed fantastically well. She was a benevolent dictator, very hands on. She was always involved in or even headed our school PTA. She simply refused to surrender her sons to a system of strangers. Her philosophy was simple: "I pay the cost to be the boss. If you turn out to be great everyone in the world will claim you, but if you turn out to be another statistic then they'll write you off and say, 'Well there goes Sylvia's boys.'" Life lessons were learned at home, be it girls, drugs, God, family, etcetera. She was our first and best teacher when it came to such matters. Our relationship was and still is very intimate. She created an environment of comfort, respectful self-expression, and opulent love. She made it clear that she was not a man and thus could not instruct us in such matters, and she was always reminding us that our family situation was not ideal: children need and are entitled to both a mother and a father.

> DID YOU HAVE A MENTOR OR A ROLE
> MODEL AS A CHILD? IF SO, DESCRIBE
> THE LESSONS AND GUIDANCE THAT
> YOU RECEIVED FROM HIM OR HER.

There were three people in particular. You know it's weird; I can look back on my life and see how God just sets things up for you. Obviously my mother was a great influence. I'm so glad that she didn't live a "double life." You know, she was not the type to say, "Do as I say and not as I do."

My older brother, who is eight years older than me, was also a role model. Although we are opposites of one another, he motivated me. He is one of the most incredible intellectuals that I know. I mean, he is the type to read world history for fun. He inspired me to appreciate wisdom and learning.

Then you have beautiful teachers—all of different hues—encouraging you. It's one thing when someone of the same race as you gives you encouragement, but to have people of different races and nationalities telling you that if you do X and Y, you will be successful. That just does something for you.

Of course we all have those bouts of solitude. We all feel, at some point, that we are alone. However, in remembering those people in my corner, I realize that I'm not alone. Everyone always likes to root for the underdog. Why? It is because he has nothing to lose. It is the person with expectations that has everything to lose. I tend to cheer for them.

I actually did have a relationship with my dad. Every boy loves his dad even if he doesn't know him. Everyone on my father's side of the family (even though I mainly saw them at funerals) would always say how much of him they saw in me. Although I really wouldn't consider him a role model, I did love him. Even in his last days, my father urged me to live out the best of him in me.

Last, but definitely not least, the "man," Dr. Walter Turnbull, founder of the Boys' Choir of Harlem. Walter, or "Doc" as we called him, was the first male who actually echoed what my mother was trying to teach me, but in a more masculine way. He was no nonsense, relatable, affirming, and brilliant.

When it comes to a mother and a son, the son can do no wrong. He could commit mass homicide, and the mother will defend her son by saying, "My son just had a bad day." Fathers are a great deal closer to the realm of reality. Everyone desires their father's blessing. It's just one of those things. A mother may carry the baby in the womb for nine months, but no matter what, your life comes from that seed that was planted by the man. While I may look like and get certain qualities from my biological father, Walter Turnbull fathered me. Spiritually and artistically, Walter was my dad. He was terrifically educated, tough, and excellent. He embodied every attribute one could hope for in a father. He would chastise us when necessary, as only a father can do, but he would also celebrate our accomplishments and/or progress. He was far more concerned about our development as men than he was our progress as musicians.

Some women will never understand that bond between a father and son, especially when it comes to discipline. I'm not sure my wife fully understands the way I discipline our son. I simply tell her, "It's a man thing." One day while outside with my son, a woman approached us and said, "I can tell he completely trusts you, he holds your hand like you're God." As young as my son is, I can sense he knows I've got his best interests at heart.

That's how I felt about Dr. Turnbull. Tragically, he died from prostate cancer. Ironically, Walter had no biological children. He was married to the choir and we were his children. He was also firmly committed to dispelling the myth of black degeneracy, through tireless discipline, encouragement, excellence, and, most importantly, character. Without character all the talent in the world is fool's gold. I am eternally grateful for my mother and Dr. Walter Turnbull.

WHAT IS YOUR CURRENT OCCUPATION? DESCRIBE THE STEPS THAT YOU HAD TO TAKE TO ARRIVE ON YOUR CURRENT CAREER PATH.

I am currently the ringmaster of Ringling Bros. and Barnum & Bailey Circus *The Greatest Show on Earth.* One of my teachers told me, "When preparation meets opportunity, shit happens." There was no plan for what I got into.

The cleaner version is that my commitment to studying voice was what gave me the opportunity with Ringling Bros. Essentially it was not of my making; this historic opportunity fell in my lap, and I just so happened to be prepared for it.

When I was presented with the Ringling Bros. opportunity, I had an important decision to make professionally: do I decline the offer and pursue a career in opera, on the stage, or some other form of music? Or do I choose history? So I chose history. History is what we're all after anyway, right? I am the first of my kind to do this—ten years before Obama! That's what I love most about what I do: everything we do as African Americans, we have the whole world watching us. White America has never had to endure that kind of pressure. Comedian Chris Rock sums it up in the movie *Head of State* (ironically, in the movie Chris plays an African American who is running for president of the United States): when a Caucasian campaign member suggests the option of quitting the presidential race, Chris's character says, "I wish I could quit. I wish it was that easy. You're lucky. You are so lucky. You don't know how good you got it. You just represent yourself. Me? I represent my whole race. If I quit there won't be another black candidate for years."

DESCRIBE THE IMPACT THAT EDUCATION HAS HAD ON YOUR LIFE.

The issue for me was the *type* of education that impacted me. The priority, for me, was artistic education. Keep in mind that everything is centered on "access." Self-education was also emphasized at home. I have always been a "work-study" type of learner. I try to learn something, then apply it; learn and do. You cannot be afraid to fall on your face sometimes. My education was two-fold: one day I was in Spanish class, the next day I was in Spain. It was an extraordinary existence.

While [I was] at school, images of Benjamin Banneker, Haile Selassie, Malcolm X, and Madame C.J. Walker—on and on—were on the walls. I was exposed to the "best of myself" through hard work and our history. What this does for you as an African American is rehab you, for lack of a better word.

In this Western Hemisphere, we are seen as strange people. We are treated differently, and this treatment is no accident. Ironically that is the reason why people want to be like us. For three thousand years in this hemisphere, we have been lied out of the Bible, lied out of history, lied out of our classrooms. What's scary is that those aforementioned great people aren't really important in general history. If we are not careful, they don't become important to you, when they should be. Author Randall Robinson said, "We must commit ourselves to rigorous scholarship." No one is going to tell your story like you can.

> IN YOUR OPINION, WHAT IS THE MAIN
> ISSUE THAT IS DISTRACTING TODAY'S
> YOUTH FROM ACHIEVING THEIR FULL
> POTENTIAL?

The trauma of knowing they are unloved. They are expressing it in a myriad of ways, be it drug use, gangs, pregnancy, or suicide pacts, America's youth know they are not loved. Their parents have sacrificed them to a system of strangers. Their parents demand that the system educate their children, yet those same parents don't show up to any PTA meetings. Most don't even vote, some aren't even registered, yet they have the audacity to expect change? We have created a society committed to *self*. Ride any public transit in New York and observe how committed passengers are to blocking each other out. We created every gadget and device imaginable to keep us distant from one another.

This is our legacy to our children. Community is not even in the vernacular. Everything is about ME. This is how we govern, we educate, we worship, and, unfortunately, how we parent.

When I hear our president give his "no excuses" speeches, telling our youth to pull themselves up by their bootstraps, pull up their pants, etcetera, it's all well and good. But telling a kid to stay in school when the school is run down, the books are outdated, the teachers don't care, and the school, at best, is designed simply to get kids to pass a test is absurd.

You cannot tell someone to go get a job when our businesses are allowed to leave the communities that built them, and some kid in Indonesia is doing my job for $10 a week, if that. You cannot tell someone to get in shape and be healthy when the produce and food in their local grocery stores is rotten, and there are no safe playgrounds for children to play or parks where they and their families can exercise and bond. It's hard to appreciate nature in a concrete jungle. The Bible declares that it means nothing to offer salutations—"peace be unto you," "God bless you"—and not fill the need(s) of that person or community. You can't breed a hopeless generation and then judge their desperation.

WHAT ADVICE DO YOU HAVE FOR A
YOUNG PERSON IN TODAY'S WORLD?

I believe P.T. Barnum said it best: "Unless a man enters upon the vocation intended for him by nature, and best suited to his peculiar genius, he cannot succeed." Go where your heart is leading you. Go the way you know to be right. I don't care where you're from or what your situation may be; we all know how to do the right thing. Do all that you can to get to where you need to be and doors you've never thought possible will open. Create your own sphere of influence. If you're surrounded by ne'er-do-wells, then get an imaginary friend. Live your life like it matters, but first and foremost you must believe that you indeed matter and that no one in the history of the world can be you or do what you have been designed to do.

WERE THERE ANY OBSTACLES IN YOUR LIFE THAT YOU HAD TO OVERCOME? HOW DID YOU HURDLE THEM?

It's hard to touch on one specific thing. Fatherlessness was a hurdle, but I didn't have it like most kids have it. I had beautiful surrogates, my godfather, the Boys Choir of Harlem, etcetera, so I never had time to contemplate my father not being there.

The perpetual obstacle is self. The greatest obstacle for me is removing myself, getting out of my own way, and letting "thy will be done." I think that is the hardest thing for humanity to do. I have no control over what is and what will be; all I can do is put my hand to the plow and work.

WHAT DOES FAMILY MEAN TO YOU?

Purpose. A man's paradigm is power, significance. We "do," we "conquer," we "pursue"—that is our makeup. A man's life is powered by purpose. Women desire this in a man because her paradigm is security. Holidays, birthdays, and anniversaries mean nothing to us as men. I've never heard a man bemoan not receiving any gifts on Valentine's Day. Most men don't even know when Father's Day is. Holidays, birthdays, and anniversaries matter to us because it matters to our wives and children. Family gives us purpose. Purpose is what makes everything matter.

HOW DO YOU GIVE BACK TO YOUR COMMUNITY?

Mind your business. I give to my community by perfecting myself. You have to build yourself up first. In doing that I am able to build up my family. I am responsible for the condition of my family. The children I produce and the wife I love will either shine or be a hindrance to the community based on what they receive from me.

If we would just "mind our own business": husbands being husbands, fathers being fathers, wives being wives—not their husband's mothers—everything in the world would be better off. It's that simple. There would be no degenerate children, gang violence, or police brutality because criminals and dishonorable police officers would understand that they would be dealing with active fathers in those communities and would certainly think twice about harming their children. Accountability is what sustains and even elevates a community.

| WHAT IS YOUR PHILOSOPHY ON LIFE?

Love! There is nothing else. Every pursuit, every accomplishment, every set back, without love it means nothing. 1 Corinthians 13:1–3 is the truest thing ever written. Governments, religions, laws, families, talents, education, etcetera, all fail. For without love, the aforementioned are frustrated shells of the human imagination. But it is in love and through love that all things are perfected.

Governments are neither established nor maintained by military might nor opulent wealth, but from the loving and active will of the people. Religion, with its holy sacraments and rituals, accounts for nothing without a heart lovingly bent toward justice, mercy, and truth. Without love laws are hollow legalized burdens that lack the power to edify or change the offender. Without love a family is merely a house of strangers, talents lie dormant and unfulfilled, and education is empty and often dangerous, since scholarship can be used to serve one's whims. Love is all.

CHAPTER 5

A FUTURE LEADER
NOW

(You Are Never Too Young To "Do You")

Just when I thought I was done with this book, Darren Jackson came along. While at a black Greek picnic (Darren is a member of Omega Psi Phi Fraternity, Inc.), I overheard Darren talking about his immediate school and career plans to a group of friends and was immediately impressed with his ambition, talent, and overall passion for improving the lives of others. Upon eavesdropping on his plans to go abroad to Senegal in order to study the disparity of their health care system relative to health care systems in more developed nations, I asked him if he would like to be a part of *Beyond the Statistics*.

At twenty-three years old, Darren has committed himself to higher education, attending prestigious institutions from Morgan State to Columbia University. Eventually Darren plans on attending Yale Medical School en route to becoming one of the top health care professionals in the world. Talking with him makes me feel like I can do more to improve the lives of others in the best way that I know how, which is telling stories of inspiration and sharing my experiences with others. He is the youngest person that I interviewed for this project, yet he seems like the oldest because he is wise beyond his years and has done more for others in his few years in this world than many have done in their lifetimes.

Darren, who may well be on his way to becoming the U.S. surgeon general one day, proves that where you grew up does not necessarily dictate your success level. You can be a positive and dominant force in the world, whether you come from "the hood" or the suburbs.

DARREN JACKSON, FULL-TIME STUDENT

Young Darren Jackson on his way to mentor at
Harlem Children's Zone.

| **WHAT IS YOUR AGE?**

Although many have said that I have an old soul, I am twenty-five years young.

| **WHERE ARE YOU FROM? TELL ME ABOUT YOUR "ROOTS."**

They call it the place where dreams are made, and I would truly have to agree. I am a New Yorker, native to Hempstead Long Island. At the age of sixteen I was blessed with the opportunity to begin college at Morgan State University in Baltimore, Maryland. So in part I can attribute a great deal of my development to the "charm city."

Both sides of my family are American-born blacks, my mother's side from the South and my father's from the northeast. I was raised in what you would call a Southern Baptist household. Although my parents were separated and I mainly lived with my mother, both of my parents played a major role in my upbringing.

| **WHAT IMPACT DID YOUR LIVING ENVIRONMENT HAVE ON YOUR CHILDHOOD?**

A child's environment and upbringing have major implications on the way he or she may mature into adulthood. It is well known that the frontal lobe of the brain reaches full maturity around the age of twenty-five. Because the frontal lobe is responsible for cerebral processes ranging from long-term memory to motivational drive, my surroundings during these years were key in my development.

I faced typical adolescent obstacles during my childhood, such as gangs and drugs. I've seen many friends get sucked into very unproductive lifestyles. I call it the "here and now" mentality: individuals getting caught up in fast lifestyles and not understanding that there are opportunities beyond the neighborhood. Some say that your environment defines you, and often that is used as an excuse to explain malice and unproductive behavior. However, I used bad examples in my surroundings to represent the direct opposite of what I wanted to be. I couldn't imagine letting ten years pass me by, living in the same "hood" and hanging around the same unproductive individuals. It haunted me. It gave me the drive to double up eleventh and twelfth grade so that I could experience different environments and cultures.

> DID YOU HAVE A ROLE MODEL OR
> MENTOR AS A CHILD? IF SO, DESCRIBE
> THE LESSONS AND GUIDANCE THAT
> YOU RECEIVED FROM HIM OR HER.

It takes a village to raise a child, right? So I had many role models. I can think of so many teachers, neighbors, and church family members that provided me with guidance throughout the years. My mother taught me to be organized and to follow through with tasks. My dad always schooled me on self-presentation with his well-known saying, "When you go out, first you represent yourself, then your family, and finally your race." However, if I had to choose one person that I feel kept me motivated throughout the years, I would have to say it was my oldest sister, Kim. She is very motivated and driven. She went to summer school in order to graduate from high school early, so I did the same. She went to Howard at a young age, so I went to Morgan at a young age. She majored in political science, pre-law, so I majored in biology, pre-med. It was inherent sibling competition that kept me going. Mind you, there was never any bad blood or ill-willed rivalry, but because she set the bar pretty high with every step she took in her education, I was compelled to do the same.

| WHAT IS YOUR CURRENT OCCUPATION? DESCRIBE THE STEPS THAT YOU HAD TO TAKE TO ARRIVE ON YOUR CURRENT CAREER PATH.

I am a full-time student; there is no eloquent way to state that. I just completed my graduate studies at the Mailman School of Public Health at Columbia University, and I am currently applying to medical school. I am not employed in the sense of going to work and receiving a salary; however, I am employed in terms of the time I dedicate to furthering my education. At this point I am so used to the daily rigor of a student's lifestyle that it doesn't bother me. It almost feels as if there is no other way to live. Even though I know my lifestyle will change soon—and that time and hour is very uncertain—school keeps me on my toes. It is a daily balance of time management, decision-making, and perseverance.

Outside of schoolwork, I also participate in research at the New York Neurological Institute's stroke division at the Columbia University medical campus. In this research I am studying social disparities affecting stroke victims in a multi-ethnic population in Northern Manhattan (Washington Heights). This work is very rewarding because my interest in public health is heavily geared toward socio-economic and racial disparities of health. I plan on using my degree in public health, combined with my medical training, to target specific populations that are vulnerable to these disparities and help develop effective prevention and intervention methods for these individuals. Health is a human right, and I pray my work will be a catalyst to healthier lifestyles, especially within minority and under-served communities.

DESCRIBE THE IMPACT THAT EDUCATION HAS HAD ON YOUR LIFE.

This is simple: education has a major impact on my life. Education equips me with the tools I need to effectively perform in my field. With that, coupled with my God-given drive, I am able to succeed in all that I do.

I come from a public school background. From there I attended a public, historically black university, Morgan State University, and most recently a private Ivy League institution, Columbia University. Every step of my education was a lesson to be learned. My education was not just academic; it also fine-tuned my overall character. People often forget about the social aspect of education. It becomes so one-dimensional and cliché. It's not just about books, going to class, listening to long lectures, and spending the remainder of the evening in the library. It also involves the people you meet, the experiences you have, and the networks you make. All of this ties into education. You can't have one without the other. Achieving excellence in academics at the expense of social skills leaves a student with a major disadvantage.

> ## IN YOUR OPINION, WHAT IS THE MAIN ISSUE THAT IS DISTRACTING YOUTH TODAY FROM ACHIEVING THEIR FULL POTENTIAL?

I can only speak about what I see in my neighborhoods. This is my opinion about underserved communities, and even then my statements are not meant to be generalized to every minority population. This question brings me back to the "here and now" mentality I spoke about previously. I believe that many of today's youth are too concentrated on what's "poppin" now to be concerned with long-term goals and outcomes. This doesn't mean that they lack ambition; it's just that many of them feel as though they are forever young. I am not sure if this is a result of the times or simply a conventional issue faced by adolescents across all generations. One thing is for sure: the proper reinforcement to minimize these vices is absent within the homes, schools, and neighborhoods.

This is a multi-level issue. It encompasses more than just what's plaguing the youth. It's more about the downfall of society. Society has failed our youth, and then in turn society expects the youth to thrive in a flawed system. The school system is broken, and the modern family unit is also shattered. The elders are not respected as such, the church is no longer the cornerstone of the community, and the majority of entertainers and media figures are not setting a high bar of achievement like the leaders of the past. I am not blaming celebrities for the poor decisions of young people, but let's face it: this is a "watch and repeat" media-driven society. If children grow up in a society where people they emulate and identify with preach messages of unity, self-evolution, and empowerment, then those are tenants the youth might work toward. On the other hand, if "hood" tales of malice, gang violence, and drugs are constantly lauded, then maybe these are the things the youth would embrace. However, excuses are tools of incompetence and should not be used to downplay the accountability of an individual for his or her own actions.

As I stated before, the issues plaguing the youth of today are multi-dimensional. It would take more time than we can afford to remedy every dimension of these issues. After everything is said and done, I feel as though the fastest and most effective resolve rests on the youth. They must know who they are and not be so easily swayed by social norms. If this is imbedded in the youth, whether inherently or by outside conditioning, there will be an abandonment of mediocrity, which seems to be the standard of our time. This abandonment of mediocrity will usher in a new attitude of excellence amongst our youth.

WHAT ADVICE DO YOU HAVE FOR
A YOUNG PERSON GROWING UP IN
TODAY'S WORLD?

I am a religious person, so I would start off by saying always keep God first, knowing that through him anything is possible. Enjoy life, but always keep in mind an ultimate goal. Set a high bar of achievement and stop at nothing to conquer your dreams. It may sound corny, but you must operate with the same tenacity a hungry cheetah uses to hunt prey. Stay hungry. Never accept an obstacle as a roadblock but as a hurdle that must be exploded through.

WERE THERE ANY OBSTACLES IN YOUR
LIFE THAT YOU HAD TO OVERCOME?
HOW DID YOU HURDLE THEM?

I think the obstacles I faced growing up were no different from my peer group's. The neighborhood had gangs and drugs and the school systems were not the best, but I still managed to make it work for me. Outside of the normal childhood pressures, I honestly feel that I didn't have too much adversity to overcome during my upbringing, which is truly a blessing. God provided me with a strong family unit, church family, and teachers that valued their jobs.

WHAT DOES FAMILY MEAN TO YOU?

My family means everything to me. My family is not only biological, but it includes my friends as well. In the same respect, I also consider my family to be my friends. My fraternity's motto states that "friendship is essential to the soul," and this saying can be inclusive of all relationships an individual holds dear to his or her heart. Family and friends gave me a strong foundation to achieve success and because of them, coupled with my unwavering faith in God, I was able to go farther in life than I ever imagined.

HOW DO YOU GIVE BACK TO YOUR COMMUNITY?

As I mentioned before, I am currently conducting social disparity research to increase the knowledge of specific issues contributing to an increased burden of disease in underserved communities in an effort to promote healthier lifestyles. Within my international pursuits for health promotion, I sit on the board of directors for the Kendeya Community Health Partnership (KCHP). KCHP is a community-based organization based in Saraya, Senegal, which is in the southeastern region of the country. In KCHP our primary mission is to improve the overall access to health care by building on the capacity of both the government health services and of the local communities of Senegal. We know that by reinforcing health education, improving government health facilities, implementing community nutrition and sanitation programs and infectious disease initiatives, we will be able to improve health issues that are central across the entire country.

I am also very active within my fraternity (Omega Psi Phi Fraternity Inc.), in which I serve as the current vice basileus of my graduate chapter in Brooklyn, New York. We have conducted social action programs such as blood drives and enrichment programs targeting high school youth. I am also planning a major conference to be held at my alma mater, Morgan State, called *Restoring, Uplifting, Leadership, Education, Success (R.U.L.E.S.) for Black Men Symposium.* For this symposium my home chapter of Omega, Pi chapter, and I will be inviting out minority male leaders from just about every field to meet with young men from all over the northeast. Our mission is to address obstacles unique to underrepresented male groups through collaborative building and networking by way of activism and social accountability within our campus and surrounding communities. We feel that every young man can gain empowerment through group learning, building, and, most importantly, brotherhood.

WHAT IS YOUR PHILOSOPHY ON LIFE?

My philosophy on life comes from what my father used to tell me throughout my childhood. He said, "Wayne, in life, you can be two things to someone, either an asset or a liability." Every day you should wake up thinking about the change you can be not only for yourself but for those around you as well. Think about how your actions can affect another's life. Will it be for the better or will it be for the worse? Will you be an asset to their lives or a liability?

CHAPTER 6

HUMBLE
BEGINNINGS

LAMECK "HUMBLE" LUKANGA

Humble, dressed for success.

hen I think about my life growing up in Harlem, New York, I felt that I had it very difficult as a kid. Sometimes I felt as though I had to be a parent to my own mother as she battled her demons. At times, I felt alone and unloved by family or friends. However, when a good friend of mine introduced me to Lameck "Humble" Lukanga, it changed my perspective of what difficult truly was. At the age 26, Humble has solidified himself as one of the top financial professionals in the sports and entertainment industry, representing some very high profile clients. Just to think, that just twenty years ago, Humble did not think he would make it to see the age of seven. More important than the success he has attained, Humble is a true lover of humanity, who cares with honesty and compassion. I present to you, Humble's testimony of faith, hope and love.

| WHAT IS YOUR AGE?

I'm 26 years young.

| WHERE ARE YOU FROM? TELL ME
| ABOUT YOUR "ROOTS."

I'm from Uganda, a small country in East Africa. I grew up in a humble village called Masaka, where I found my childhood full of genocide, 3rd world poverty, famine and disease. The conditions that I grew up in were very severe, I remember having to walk miles every day in hopes of finding water for the elders in the village. I come from very humble beginnings. My father, who was an educator, was able to get us political asylum when the conditions became too harsh to bare. I came to the United States at age 11 ½, which then changed the entire trajectory of my life.

WHAT IMPACT DID YOUR LIVING ENVIRONMENT HAVE ON YOUR CHILDHOOD?

The impact of my environment meant I didn't get a chance to have a childhood; I don't really remember playing or toys or anything we attribute to being children. You are forced to grow up fast and become responsible for everyone around you at an early age. By the age of six or seven, you are cooking, hunting, babysitting and providing whatever is needed for the elders. Seventy-five percent of children were dying during infancy due to the living conditions, so just being alive to see six or seven years of life was a true miracle.

DID YOU HAVE A ROLE MODEL OR MENTOR AS A CHILD? IF SO, DESCRIBE THE LESSONS AND GUIDANCE THAT YOU RECEIVED FROM HIM OR HER.

My role model was my father. He was a mountain of a man. My father decided very early in his life that he would lead a life of service, and his worth would be measured by how many people he was able to help. My father was a mountain of a man! He was really bright, got a chance to get his bachelor's degree in Economics at the University of Nairobi in Kenya. His intellectual ability got him an opportunity to go to University of Southern California, where he got his masters degree in Public Administration. After receiving his masters, he went right back to the same village I was eventually born in and taught everyone he could about business, finance, and economics. He helped farmers, merchants and politicians start initiatives that helped everyone survive droughts, famine, and disease. My father loved his people and was a man of integrity, with a heart full of compassion. I've tried my whole life to grow to be a mirror of who he was. I lost my father in August of 2009, but the greatest lesson he taught me that lives in my heart is that individual success doesn't mean anything if it doesn't lead to collective progress.

> WHAT IS YOUR CURRENT
> OCCUPATION? DESCRIBE THE STEPS
> THAT YOU HAD TO TAKE TO ARRIVE
> ON YOUR CURRENT CAREER PATH.

I'm a Business Manager for professional athletes and entertainers, where my major role is to manage their finances and business affairs. I essentially become the CFO of every client we represent, and it's a huge responsibility to make sure they all succeed. I knew at an early age that I wanted to grow to be like my father. Had we stayed in Uganda, I would have been teaching farmers, merchants and public officials as well about finance and economics. However, during my college years, I started to educate myself on the sports and entertainment industries and I saw that nearly 80% of these talented people were going broke, filing bankruptcy, or in financial distress 3 to 5 years after they retired. I wanted to change these statistics. In a small way, I felt that I could be like my father by educating them on how to manage their finances and affairs so they could turn around and impact their families, communities, and eventually, the world. I've dedicated my life to this purpose and so far it's been a real blessing.

DESCRIBE THE IMPACT THAT EDUCATION HAS HAD ON YOUR LIFE.

Education has been the driving force in all that I've been able to accomplish. Where I grew up, school was a luxury, not a born right. Very few people had access to a formal education, so when I came to the U.S., I was shocked to find that school was free. In addition to that, they sent a bus to pick you up, provided free lunch and would give you textbooks to read for the whole year, I was blown away. I have never taken the opportunity to sit in any classroom for granted and that dedication has made all the difference for me.

IN YOUR OPINION, WHAT IS THE MAIN ISSUE THAT IS DISTRACTING YOUTH TODAY FROM ACHIEVING THEIR FULL POTENTIAL?

The main issue distracting kids these days are the broken family structures. The man is no longer in the home, the mother can't help with the homework because she's working night and day to provide. Our communities don't parent each other's children, and once the foundation is broken, what can you truly build from it? We have to strengthen our families again, we have to care about the neighbor's child as well, and we have to be a community of purpose-driven people and get rid of the individualistic way of life. Our children are looking outside of their homes for love, guidance and acceptance. If we fail to rebuild our families, we will fail our children.

| WHAT ADVICE DO YOU HAVE FOR
| A YOUNG PERSON GROWING UP IN
| TODAY'S WORLD?

My advice is very simple when I speak to young people, "Be Good and Do Good". If you can follow those simple words, you will create a positive lifestyle, which over time will yield positive results in any arena you choose to be a part of. Every single day, you wake up and you be good and you do good. We as humans complicate life. It is really a simple formula.

| WERE THERE ANY OBSTACLES IN YOUR
| LIFE THAT YOU HAD TO OVERCOME?
| HOW DID YOU HURDLE THEM?

As I eluded to earlier, I grew up in civil wars, poverty stricken environments, famine and disease. My entire life was an obstacle that only few overcame. I've been to more funerals for loved ones than years I've been alive. It hasn't been an easy road and I thank God for that. I overcame every obstacle by never feeling sorry for myself. I understand deeply that life isn't made to be easy, it's made to be meaningful. Throughout the journey of life, no one goes unhurt, but how you respond to adversity is the measure of your own character. Everything I've ever experienced gave me a new appreciation for the air in my lungs. So everyday above ground is a great one, because the latter is much worse than anything stressing that I have going on.

WHAT DOES FAMILY MEAN TO YOU?

Family to me is the foundation of life. Who we become, what we fear, what we understand, what we accept, what we reject, what we see of ourselves come from who we are as a family. If we strengthen the family structures, we strengthen the world.

HOW DO YOU GIVE BACK TO YOUR COMMUNITY?

I teach, teach, and teach. I'm always at a community center, learning institutions from middle school to universities teaching. I hold seminars in my office, I hold phone lectures, I'm always teaching. I believe that you are never too young to teach or never too old to learn. We must put a piece of ourselves in every person we meet.

| WHAT IS YOUR PHILOSOPHY ON LIFE?

My philosophy in life is: may all living beings be free from suffering. I want everyone to live a happy life, and I have to do my part. That is each of our greatest responsibility to each other. Keep in mind, you owe more to the human race than you do to any country that you were born in. You are a human being first before you are an American, African, European, etcetera. Let's love one another and bring peace and understanding to each other so our children can have a world that they can be proud of.

CHAPTER 7

ABOUT THE AUTHOR
(I'm As Successful As The Company I Keep)

Perhaps one of the hardest things to do is to write about oneself, especially when I feel that my achievements pale in comparison to my peers in this book. At heart I feel like a regular guy: one who goes to work, comes home, and enjoys his family, and one who just wants the best for others and himself. Maybe my positive mindset is due to all of these powerful influences that God has placed in my life. He allowed me access to peers that are doing great things, so it was difficult to "become a statistic" because I was always given a blueprint to follow by my friends, teachers, and some family members.

I didn't have a consistent father figure in my life, but I was given a caring and compassionate mother and selfless grandmother. Whenever I felt lonely or like I was going to get caught up in the streets, recreational drugs, and other temptations, God placed teachers like Mr. Mays and friends like Kwame Ohemeng in my life. When faced with the enemy of self-doubt, he placed Wouri and Ross in my life. I saw what they were doing, and I said to myself, "I may not be able to do what they do, but I can still do my thing." When I was feeling tired, run-down, and defeated, he put Josh and Johnathan into my life, and they infused me with new energy. After hearing and knowing their stories personally, I knew I could muster the energy necessary to put this project together. Thank you all, for all that you've said and done and for all that you are. A part of each and every one of you lives in me.

Zane M. Massey, Finance Professional and entrepreneur

A picture of me, taken by my wife, at Ross's wedding.

| WHAT IS YOUR AGE?

I'm a young thirty-four years old.

WHERE ARE YOU FROM? TELL ME
ABOUT YOUR "ROOTS."

My late grandmother, Vivian, who was the head of our family, was born in Jacksonville, Florida. Her descendents were Native American, African, and Irish. This ambitious woman often scrubbed the steps of row houses to make a dollar while growing up in Baltimore, Maryland. Her ambitious spirit propelled her to New York City, where she became a licensed practical nurse. My grandmother retired from the Department of Health, where she was a public health assistant for more than twenty years. However, I remember her going off to her second job, private duty nursing, which she did well into her seventies. She supported her three children with the help of my great-grandmother, Fannie. During her lifetime my grandmother managed to purchase her own home in the Bronx in the 1950s and a cooperative apartment in Queens in the 1960s. In the mid 1970s she realized her dream when she had a home built in Shokan, New York. My grandmother was always ahead of her time, wise, and intuitive. She is sorely missed.

I was born in upstate New York in a town called Kingston to an African American mother and a Jewish father. Kingston is a relatively rural area, about ninety minutes outside of New York City. People commute from there for work, but I wouldn't want to do it. I lived there for all of two years with my grandmother and other extended family while my mom was in the military. When she returned we moved to Harlem. At the time my mother and grandmother maintained separate apartments in Harlem. During my childhood my mom and I moved several times. I once lived in Baltimore, Maryland, with my Aunt Joyce for a whole year. This was when I was about seven or eight; I can't quite remember. By the time I was a teenager, I had moved about four times within the Harlem, New York, area.

WHAT IMPACT DID YOUR LIVING ENVIRONMENT HAVE ON YOUR CHILDHOOD?

My living environment had a great impact on me, both positively and negatively. Growing up in Harlem at the height of the "Reaganomics Era" was tough on most people of color living in inner-city areas. This period was characterized by the popularity of crack-cocaine and the spread of HIV/AIDS. I can remember, as a fourth- and fifth-grader, walking to school in the morning (which was about five minutes from home) and counting crack vials that were on the ground. I became aware of prostitutes at an early age, since many people labeled as "crack-heads" lived in my building. I was never exposed to them firsthand, but I remember several of them would do "favors" for some of the older gentlemen that lived in my neighborhood.

While my living environment had a lot of negative aspects to it, I was exposed to some of the most loving and genuine people in the world. In the midst of growing up in the "hood," I always had family and friends in the neighborhood looking after me. If my mom wasn't around, it seemed as though I was always with a cousin, uncle, or aunt. Since I was exposed at an early age to the negative situations that life can bring, I was "scared straight" into doing the right thing, which meant stay in school and excel—by any means necessary.

> ### DID YOU HAVE A MENTOR OR A ROLE
> ### MODEL AS A CHILD? IF SO, DESCRIBE
> ### THE LESSONS AND GUIDANCE THAT
> ### YOU RECEIVED FROM HIM OR HER.

My grandmother was one of the most prominent role models in my life. She was tough but could be exceptionally caring and loving. She is the only woman I have ever been afraid of—with the exception of my wife. She instilled in me the necessary mental toughness I would need to survive in this often-cruel world. There was something about her philological approach to life that taught me to appreciate every single day on earth. Whether she was working twenty-four-hour shifts at the hospital or cooking a flavorful and soulful meal, she would always put her best foot forward. I remember she would take my cousin Josette and me shopping at the "junk shop," where she would search endlessly for bargains in clothing and food for us. My shirts, although they were purchased for fifty cents, were always ironed and freshly creased, courtesy of her. The price-reduced canned goods and meat were converted into wonderful meals full of love. She taught me to always appreciate what I have and to thank God for every breath that I take.

As a different kind of role model, my mother taught me that all things are possible as long as you have the will to survive. Throughout the late 1980s and early 1990s, my single mother battled an addiction to crack-cocaine while raising me in Harlem. Today she is a successful substance-abuse counselor with a master's degree in social work. She always tells me that I was the reason she wanted to continue living, but honestly, she is the reason why I want to continue my life's journey. She taught me that perseverance really does pay off. I actually look at her life as a modern day miracle. Her life truly makes me feel that I can do *anything* that I want to do.

The last person I consider a role model is my fifth grade teacher, Mr. Phillip Mays. Mays made me feel special. *He told me that I was special.* Although I was only ten or eleven years old at the time, he would stay after school with me, playing basketball and just talking about life. He spoke to me like I was an adult, often telling me of the obstacles I would have to ultimately overcome as a black man, such as poverty, racism, and social inequality. Besides giving me the confidence that I could excel in any classroom, he prepared me for the real world that was soon to come. The icing on the cake was that this man, who I looked up to so much, named his first-born son after me.

Every man needs a Mr. Mays-type of person to push him along. No one does it all by themselves. I like to compare Mr. Mays to a "corner-man" in boxing. A fighter, no matter how much talent he may have, is only as good as his corner-man. If there is no corner-man urging him to continue, giving him instructions, nourishing the fighter with water, and applying Vaseline over cuts, the fighter will lose. The corner-man has to do all of these things; all the fighter has to do is fight. Emmanuel Steward is one of the most prolific trainers/corner-men in the sport of boxing, having elevated fighters such as Lennox Lewis and Vladimir Klitscho to the heavyweight championship of the world. Mr. Mays was my Emmanuel Steward in life.

WHAT IS YOUR CURRENT
OCCUPATION? DESCRIBE THE STEPS
THAT YOU HAD TO TAKE TO ARRIVE
ON YOUR CURRENT CAREER PATH.

I am currently a senior financial analyst for a global health care firm. I work within the Controller's Department, which oversees the budgeting and forecasting operations of the business as well as the analysis of our competitors. I am an entrepreneur as well, with interests in writing, real estate, and fashion.

DESCRIBE THE IMPACT THAT
EDUCATION HAS HAD ON YOUR LIFE.

Education has given me access to places and people that I would not have been exposed to otherwise. In the professional world, it seems that people regard you based on three criteria: how you look, your level of education, and what you actually know. By going to the right school, you give yourself a greater chance for a better quality of life. There are bright people out there who probably don't need to go to school, such as your Kanye Wests, Jay-Zs, entrepreneurs like Farrah Gray, etcetera. These people already have "it." But my education has leveled the playing field, allowing me to play on the same level that people of other hues, backgrounds, and ethnicities play on.

Education has also strengthened my ability to deal with diversity. Business is conducted on a global scale. A typical college classroom, filled with kids from various backgrounds and countries, is the "new normal". In business school, the very people that I sat next to or in front of, represent the people that I currently work with - people from Germany, Asia, Africa, and all over the world. The more you can adapt to and work with people of different backgrounds, the more valuable you can become in business. Had I not pursued higher education, my reality would have only encompassed my Harlem neighborhood. Since many of my family members were not given the opportunities that I have been afforded, I feel that it would have been criminal not to educate myself, whether in the classroom or in the real world.

> IN YOUR OPINION, WHAT IS THE MAIN
> ISSUE THAT IS DISTRACTING YOUTH
> TODAY FROM ACHIEVING THEIR FULL
> POTENTIAL?

I honestly think that some of the same pressures (lack of a family structure, peer pressure, pursuit of the material over morals, one's perception of him or herself) youth face today are no different from what has happened throughout history. I have been reading *Race and Economics* by the famous African American economist Thomas Sowell. In his book, published in 1975, Sowell basically highlights the fact that a lot of homes were without fathers, children were growing up in poverty and under hard circumstances, and that economic resources were limited in poor communities much like they are today. While this still remains a reality in many poor communities, the main difference between today and thirty to fifty years ago, is that as the youth are getting wiser, they are getting weaker. The same human tendencies are at work, but there is now more to pursue.

As technology becomes more advanced, the clothes become more expensive, the drugs become more powerful, the diseases become more plentiful, our wills—of both youth and adults—have become weaker. The youth are just a reflection of the adults. Simply put, as we have become more sophisticated, we have become devoid of character.

WHAT ADVICE DO YOU HAVE FOR A YOUNG PERSON IN TODAY'S WORLD?

Do not feed into anyone's negative energy. If you feel that someone or something is bad for you, then move away from it. Remember that energy is never lost, it is simply transferred. It's as simple as that.

WERE THERE ANY OBSTACLES IN YOUR LIFE THAT YOU HAD TO OVERCOME? HOW DID YOU HURDLE THEM?

While growing up, I experienced the pain of watching my mother take drugs. I did everything in my power to try to stop her. However, I couldn't. As I grew older (and hopefully a little wiser), I realized that you can not change a person: he or she has to want to change. I also realized that encouraging my mother—through my words and actions—really meant something to her. Ultimately through a lot of prayer and encouragement, she was able to get sober and is now a vital asset to her community through her service as a counselor. My mother and I have a strong relationship after all that we've been through. The ups, downs, and in-betweens make us who we are. I was able to overcome this obstacle through keeping my head up, staying positive, and being the best person that I could be. You never know who is watching you. Sometimes you are able to provide a glimmer of hope to someone else through just being yourself.

| WHAT DOES FAMILY MEAN TO YOU?

Family means a great deal to me. As has been previously said, family does not have to necessarily be a blood relative. Just having an advocate—someone in your corner—can mean the world to a person. Having an extended family of teachers and peers honestly saved my life. In fact some of the people included in this book are the very reason I write these words today.

| HOW DO YOU GIVE BACK TO YOUR COMMUNITY?

Primarily I give back to my community by trying my best to be a loving husband and father. Husbands are supposed to love their wives more than anything else. An investment in one's family is the beginning of an investment in the overall community. I also am an active member of my local graduate chapter of my fraternity, Phi Beta Sigma Fraternity, Incorporated. I recently took part in the holiday toy drive for children and a health fair directed at screening men of color for different types of cancer.

| WHAT IS YOUR PHILOSOPHY ON LIFE?

I always find myself quoting Malcolm X in my head, saying, "Concerning non-violence, it is criminal to teach a man not to defend himself when he is the constant victim of brutal attacks." I took Malcolm's quote to mean the following: if you have been abused or taken advantage of, don't just sit there and continue being the victim. Arm yourself—with education, understanding, a healthier lifestyle, and a few boxing classes! Just fight back and never settle for less.

CONCLUSION

I may not write in the dynamic style of, say, a Dr. Brian Purnell, but my style may be more suitable for what needs to be said. My brothers, we are dealing with a bleak situation. We are living in a world where people no longer care about others. While we live in a world that is far more technologically advanced than those that came before us, we are just as, if not more, susceptible to dying from disease, poverty, and senseless violence than ever before. While enormous strides in the battle for racial and social equality amongst Caucasians and people of color (all non-Caucasians) have been made, culminating in the first appointment of a fully recognized African American president of the United States of America, there is still a lot of work that needs to be done.

Young men of color, particularly those of African American and Latino descent, are victims of neglect by their households, communities, and the education system. When will we realize that if we don't take care of our own, then no one will take care of us? If you are a parent, be a parent; if you are a teacher, then be a teacher; and if you can help someone out other than yourself, then please do so. If you add value to someone's life, then you have made a difference and are truly living life. We need to try to restore some of our old values that were present in our neighborhoods leading up to the time of the crack epidemics of the 1980s, when the village actually did care about the child.

Young men, do not discount yourself; whether you choose to believe it or not, you come from greatness: a long line of warriors, kings, freedom fighters, doctors, lawyers, economists, and teachers. To you young brothers out there, I say pull your damn pants up, tie your sneakers, and let's get it poppin'!

Demographics do not necessarily determine and/or limit personal potential. Racial profiling, by its nature, eliminates the best of the human spirit and psyche. There is an underlying theme present in today's Western philosophy that makes one think they are unable to go beyond the statistics, beyond their present living conditions, and beyond their existing train of thought. Do not let where you come from solely determine who you are. As I write this, some young mind is rewriting history. Some young mind will change the course of history by unveiling the cure for HIV, cancer, and the common cold. Hopefully someone reads this book and decides to be that next agent of change—the next teacher, lawyer, doctor, parent, or community spokesperson. If one person accepts his or her greatness as a result of my endeavor, then I have attained my goal. Dare to change history by changing yourself and your circumstances. Go "beyond the statistics."

SUGGESTED READING FOR
YOUNG MEN OF COLOR

This list, in no particular order, is actually recommended reading for anyone with an open mind; African American, Caucasian, young, old, boy, or girl. However, if you have a young son or know of a young man who may need some guidance, these are must-reads. Most of these books are considered short reads, which are ideal for our iPod and BlackBerry-carrying teens who are always on the go. They may even make a great gift for the Kindle or iPad.

1. *Race and Economics* by Thomas Sowell
2. *The Seven Spiritual Laws of Success: A Practical Guide to the Fulfillment of Your Dreams* by Deepak Chopra
3. *Breaking the Chains of Psychological Slavery* by Na'im Akbar
4. *What Black Men Should Do Now: 100 Simple Truths, Ideas, and Concepts* by K. Thomas Oglesby and Tavis Smiley
5. *Black Men, Obsolete, Single, Dangerous? The Afrikan American Family in Transition* by Haki R. Madhubuti
6. *The Autobiography of Malcolm X: As Told to Alex Haley* by Malcolm X, Alex Haley and Attallah Shabazz
7. *Gifted Hands: The Ben Carson Story* by Ben Carson and Cecil Murphey

8. *Invisible Man* by Ralph Ellison
9. *Narrative of the Life of Frederick Douglass, an American Slave* by Frederick Douglass
10. *Reallionaire: Nine Steps to Becoming Rich from the Inside Out* by Farrah Gray

BIBLIOGRAPHY

Sowell, Thomas, *Race and Economics,* New York: David McKay Company, Inc. 1975.

Shuford, Reginald. Racial Profiling in the USA. Open Society Justice Initiative: www.justiceinitiative.org. 2009.

Schlosser, E. "The Prison Industrial Complex." *The Atlantic Monthly* (Digital Edition), December 1998, www.atlantic.com.